FROM OXCARTS TO EMAILS

In their own words...

By

Nancy Ott Lynch

authorHOUSE

1663 LIBERTY DRIVE, SUITE 200
BLOOMINGTON, INDIANA 47403
(800) 839-8640
www.authorhouse.com

First published by AuthorHouse 08/17/04

ISBN: 1-4184-2551-6 (e)
ISBN: 1-4184-2552-4 (sc)

Printed in the United States of America
Bloomington, Indiana

This book is printed on acid-free paper.

FROM OXCARTS TO EMAILS

"There was a small log house with one room and an attic where (Conrad Welter) stored some of his household effects along with his good wife and eight children," ancestors wrote of the family's pioneering oxcart journey to Millbrook, New Jersey.

My great-grandmother – Conrad and Mary's only surviving daughter – was born in 1839 just a few months after the family unpacked in these cramped quarters. As the only girl in the family, Caroline's challenging life was complicated by her mother's death in childbirth. Caroline was only nine years old. Ten years later she married for the first time and moved to Pennsylvania.

After her Mom died, Caroline helped raise three younger siblings – Benjamin, Rebecca and newborn Henry. Her father and seven older brothers – Elijah, Jesse, Joseph, Jacob, Charles, Asa and Isaiah– tended crops and livestock while traveling the circuit preaching Methodism.

It's intriguing to picture Caroline, my grandfather's mother, riding in oxcarts as I fly jets and write emails just a generation or two later. Caroline's first and second wedding certificates hang on my walls, and through family documents a colorful picture of the life she led emerges. Millbrook Village, in the Delaware Water Gap, the town in which she was born, is now restored and run by the National Park Service.

A family tendency to live long and have children late in life led to this close family genealogical connection. Caroline was in her forties and Billy O. Ferrel in his fifties when my grandfather, Ralph Winfield Ferrel was born in the 1880s. Ralph was in his mid-thirties when my mother, his last child, Bettina Rose Ferrel was born.

Almost a hundred years ago, in 1908 and 1911, our ancestors wrote Caroline's family's story. The writings were intended to "Give to the descendants a brief outline in narrative form of the life and customs of the pioneer days."

But these papers also reveal proudly formal writing styles and the enormous impact of religion to our ancestors. My direct quotes from these writings give a flavor of the syntax of those times, as well.

Birth records show Mary Fulkerson Welter pregnant with Caroline as the family's oxcart bumped along the road to Millbrook. Our ancestors would never have addressed such a sensitive subject as pregnancy, and only these papers revealed Mary's condition.

Mary's death from "milk fever" shortly following the birth of her last child, Henry, is referred to briefly in the genealogical papers. In 1858, when Caroline was 19, she married W. J. Wilson of Blairstown, New Jersey and they moved to a farm in Dallas, Pennsylvania. Eventually, Caroline married William Oran Ferrel, and my grandfather Ralph Winfield Ferrel was born.

On the Ferrel side of the tale, yellowing pages on which "Billy O. Ferrel" penciled his 1911 biography lie in a crumbling family Bible.

In addition to Caroline's photo we have a picture of an elderly chin-whiskered William O. wearing a three-piece suit and 'relaxing' in a rocker on an open porch. There's also one of Caroline's fierce-looking father Conrad Welter.

One thing that cannot be overemphasized was the influence of Methodism on our ancestors. Christianity in general, and the Methodist religion in particular, governed their daily lives.

Family lore recounts that NO ONE got between Conrad and his God.

"Methodism was the largest popular religious movement between the Revolution and the Civil War, expanding on a scale that had never been seen before. It had a profound effect on the development of American culture and society, such that its impact can still be felt today," John Wigger wrote in 1998 in his book *Taking Heaven by Storm, Methodism and the Rise of Popular Christianity in America.*

Webster's 1828 Dictionary defines a "Christian" as a noun, as "a real disciple of Christ; one who believes in the truth of the Christian religion, and studies to follow the example, and obey the precepts, of Christ; a believer in Christ who is characterized by real piety."

That doesn't mean that our forefathers religion was dull or boring. Far from it. It was revolutionary.

William Oran Ferrel late in life

"Class leaders" such as Billy O. Ferrel and "licensed exhorters" such as Conrad Welter *had* to live exemplary lives. Exhorters and preacher candidates "were examined not only by the presiding elder and circuit riders but also by their class leaders and other peers who knew them well…" Wigger wrote.

"Methodists carefully watched over one another's public and private lives, and all members were required to attend a weekly small-group gathering, called a class meeting. Here their spiritual lives and temporal dealings were open to examination by their class leader, and they might also be asked to pray (confess) in public," Wigger explained.

"Disciplinary trials for the Hockhocking, Ohio, circuit from 1806 to 1815 ranged from cases of neglecting daily family worship to Sabbath breaking to adultery," Wigger cited. One preacher had his license suspended for traveling on the Sabbath.

Their religion wasn't even always socially acceptable. Wigger writes, "Far from being bland and predictable, early American Methodism was a volatile and often raucous affair, existing almost completely outside the control of the new nation's cultural, political and religious elite."

Even though they didn't know each other when they began to be active in the Methodist church, Caroline's father, her grandfather on her mother's side, John Fulkerson, and her second husband were Methodist "leaders" in their community. Billy O. Ferrel wrote in the early 1900s that he remained a class leader. Conrad never lost his exhorter's license and Fulkerson was a class leader, as well.

While there's much information on daily family life in these papers, many unanswerable questions remain.

First, how come William Oran Ferrel doesn't know whether his father David C. came from Ireland or Spain? William relates stories his father told, so he must have detected an accent. Perhaps David C. was second-generation in the United States, but the writings don't indicate that.

Secondly, Conrad Welter was described as a great orator despite his "impediments." Yet photos reveal nothing obviously physically wrong with him.

Death records finally resolved the third and most troublesome puzzle. Why did Conrad pull up his tenant farm stakes in 1839, pack up eight kids and a pregnant wife to trek to the mountains? A troubled economy at the time might have influenced him, but I believe the real reason is that Henry, Conrad's father, died that year at 104 and the family was more mobile!

Fourth, according to the records, Henry was Catholic when he emigrated to the US. I wonder how he felt about his son Conrad riding around on horseback preaching Methodism?

Fifth, and possibly most intriguing of all, is whether the fervently teatotaling Ferrel family was aware that historians called Coonrad's home the "Methodist Tavern" during the 1840s? Webster's 1828 dictionary referred to alcohol in its definition of tavern. However, after researching and interviewing some experts on the religion of the times, I learned that the early Methodists met in many places, including above stores, so the "Tavern" became slang for any site other than a church.

And there are some teasers. The only reference to Henry in the United States prior to the Revolutionary War puts him in "Wyoming" Valley, Pa. during "Indian troubles." What was he doing there?

While several anonymous ancestors authored the Welter documents, my grandfather Ralph Ferrel collected and edited the papers, entrusting them to his daughter – my mother – Bettina Rose Ferrel Ott.

My mother and her only living sister, Dorothy Elizabeth Ferrel Kenyon, were very helpful in researching this family history. Unfortunately, Ralph Ferrel's eldest daughter, Lucille Caroline Ferrel Brown, died before this project was begun.

My mother, and the late Mr. and Mrs. Charles Frantz, inspired much of my passion for our family's history.

Many thanks to my husband, Luke Lynch, for his tireless support during the research and writing of this book.

Original church burned - This is restored

Millbrook Church

WELTER FAMILY HISTORY
BACKGROUND

An aging Revolutionary War drummer boy who fathers a son at 64 and applies for a pension at 97 isn't your ordinary ancestor. But that's how Henry's described in the Welter family manuscripts.

Online sources reveal Henry's arrival in America with his father when he was five years old, and independent records reveal a Henricus Welter's birth in Prussia on the same day as Henry.

"Henry Welter came from Germany, was living in Wyoming during Indian trials," was the only cryptic comment from one of our ancestors' papers.

The only other known fact about Henry is that he was not a Hessian soldier. No reason was given for his coming here, nor what he did in his earliest years in America.

In the 1700s thousands of Germans were encouraged by "New Lander" captains to flee to America from tyrannical principalities. Emigration agents hawked advantages of living in the new world and travelers were offered a few years of indenture in exchange for fortune-making skills.

What emigrants didn't learn until they were on the docks was how poorly they would be treated, and if a family member died during the six-month voyage, their relatives had to make up the deceased's three to seven years of indenture.

According to a "Welter Family" Website, Henry arrived in 1740 when he was about five years old and served as a drummer under the name Henry Walter. The Welter family Website prints his pension application.

According to the Index of Revolutionary War Applications, a Henry Watter (or Wetter or Welter) did apply for a pension.

"(Henry) enlisted and entered the Company of Volunteers as a drummer in the month of May 1775 for the period of three years for common defense against the common enemy in the State of New Jersey, and that he enlisted or entered the service in a company at New Germantown, Hunterdon, New Jersey, under the command of Captain George Rhinehart, Lieut. John Read, and Ensign Morris Crammers, which company was attached to a Regiment under command of Col. John M. Holm of General Frelinghuysen's brigade of the New Jersey Militia," this application, presented to judge William Monroe on July 24, 1832, and printed on the "Welter Family" Website, states.

"While in service," Henry was "called to Elizabeth Town, Newark, Amboy, New Brunswick, Quarell Lawn, Middle Booth, Short Hills, Aquamanauk, Morris Town, Trenton, Springfield," the petition states, adding he received a written discharge after 1778.

Henry didn't appear himself, explaining "from bodily infirmity (he was 97 years old) he was "unable to attend the County Court, a distance of twenty miles."

"Saith he has no family record of his age but saith he was born in Germany in Europe and came to America with his father when he was about five years of age and settled in Roxbury Township," documents said.

While there is some question about whether his "infirmities" include wounds, there is no question that he saw action.

"New Jersey was an important state during the Revolutionary War because of its location near the center of the thirteen colonies and between New York City and Philadephia," statehousegirls guide to the United States says on its Website.

"Because of this, more battles were fought in New Jersey than in any other state," they said.

21

"Several important battles were fought in New Jersey, most importantly the battles of Trenton in 1776, which many consider to be the turning point of the Revolution."

Ralph Ferrel's youngest daughter Bettina Rose Ferrel Ott

My mother at Christmas 1993

HENRY WELTER THE DRUMMER BOY

Henry Welter jumped into the Revolutionary War fray shortly after the first shots were fired in the Battle of Lexington April 19, 1775.

Forty year-old Henry enlisted as a drummer, a high-profile position that often drew fire. The Revolutionary War drummer defied today's image of a very young boy. The Fife and Drum Corp was a well-respected, intrinsic part of our country's first war.

"During the Revolutionary War, each colony provided militia troops who normally had one or two fifers and drummers for each company," and "as early as July 1775 George Washington, the newly appointed commander in chief, was issuing orders concerning the instruction of fifers and drummers in the Continental Army..." according to the Arkansas School for the Blind history of the fife and drum.

"Music regulated the soldier's life in that army. A series of beats and signals performed by fifes and drums governed the soldier's every move... they told him when to get up, when to eat, and when to go to bed, and they also directed his movements in battles," the school relates.

"Henry served in the army until the war ended, and he settled in 1781 in Roxbury, New Jersey. According to our records, Henry's pension was granted in when he was 99 and he lived to be 104.

CONRAD'S EARLY LIFE

Henry was 64 years old in 1799 when Conrad was born. Conrad, who was also referred to as "Coonrad," had two brothers, Jacob and Isaac, and two sisters, Mary and Abigail.

While his childhood is a mystery, family documents say Conrad grew to be a man "highly esteemed for his Christian integrity and charitableness by all who knew him." He was "a true sympathetic friend to all who were in trouble, ever willing to lend a helping hand in time of trouble and always had a kind, encouraging word for all who sought his counsel."

When he was 21, Conrad married Mary Fulkerson, born April 18, 1768, daughter of John Fulkerson and Betsey Ogden of Kentucky. John Fulkerson came to America in 1788 and married Betsey December 4, 1809. After living a few years in Kentucky, John moved to Vienna, New Jersey.

"(John) was a lifelong member of the Methodist Church, a licensed exhorter, a Christian father and a friend to all who were in trouble and distress. He had the respect and esteem of all who knew him," ancestors relate.

His daughter Mary and Conrad set up tenant-farming for Jacob Cummins near Scholies Mountain in New Jersey. This area was known later as "Germantown," but is now referred to as "Long Valley."

Ancestors described farming challenges of the day: "There was no farm machinery, such as planters, drills, reapers, mowing machines, hayrakes, etc. For cutting the grain crops they used what was known as grain cradles, which were carried and worked by hand, cutting the grain, laying it in a swath."

"They raked it up in sheaves by hand with wooden hand rakes, ready for shocking and stacking. Grain was then taken to the barns and threshed by hand with hand flails. The grain was then put through a windmill turned by hand, and either put in graineries for the winter use, or put into sacks for the market," their kin wrote.

Conrad "lived in this location (Scholies Mountain) about eighteen years until his family grew in numbers and eight children came to bless his household," ancestors wrote.

Caroline Welter Wilson Ferrel

CONRAD SETTLES IN MILLBROOK IN 1839

The timing of Conrad's decision to uproot his pregnant wife and eight children to pioneer land in the Delaware Water Gap was most likely influenced by the death of his father Henry that year at 104.

"About this time, in the year 1839, having accumulated a small portion of this world's goods, sufficient for the present needs of himself and family, he began to look around for a suitable place to make a permanent home for his family," his family wrote 100 years later.

"There was a small, log house with one room and an attic where (Conrad) stored some of his household effects, with his good wife and eight children. The two hundred acres he bought was all heavily timbered. There being only a small garden spot cleared and ready for cultivation," the narrative continued.

On April 1, 1839, three months before Caroline's July 11th birth, this land was conveyed by deed from Jacob Cummins and his wife to Conrad Welter and his wife.

Conrad was "one of the first pioneers and settlers of this part of the state, a wilderness of woods with the Blue Mountains on the East, and the Delaware Mountains on the West, being one mile from the river."

He settled in a "narrow valley in one place over one and a half miles wide and in others just about wide enough for a wagon road and a small stream." The valley gradually widened until it came to a stop at the Delaware Water Gap.

"When Conrad moved to this new home across the Blue Mountains, with one or two of his old neighbors, and with ox teams and lumber wagons, a distance of twenty miles over the rough mountain road, almost the entire distance through the wilderness, the reader of this narrative can imagine what his feeling must have been to take his family away from all civilization, away from schools and churches, into this vast wilderness of mountains and woods, to begin life over again," our ancestors wrote.

While they don't give the exact route Conrad took, it is more than likely the family traveled along "The Old Mine Road" which dead-ends in the Delaware Water Gap.

"The Old Mine Road, considered the first road in America designed for wheeled vehicles, was built three hundred years ago by Dutch settlers for access to the mines of the Minisink Country," C. Gilbert. Hines wrote.

"A small nearby stream was called 'Millbrook' by Abraham Garris, who built a small flour mill in 1840 at the head of this valley. He used the water from this stream to turn the wheels of his mill to manufacture the farmer's grain into flour."

CG Hines called it "a very pleasant companion as it ambles along down its little valley, until it takes to jumping the rocks, when it sounds from the road as though it was going all to smash; however, we catch it a little later dodging under the highway in such manner as would indicate that it can be entirely cheerful under the most adverse conditions."

"The little town that afterwards sprang up there was also called Millbrook. This stream came from the mountains, having its source about two miles from Millbrook Village, and gathering its forces from many small mountain rivulets, until it reached the Delaware River, about four miles above the Water Gap."

"...On this brook there was a crude saw mill, built about the same year the flour mill was built, by a man named Enos Hill. Here the farmers and woodsmen would draw their logs with ox teams and have them manufactured into such sizes

and shapes as were necessary for their building purposes."

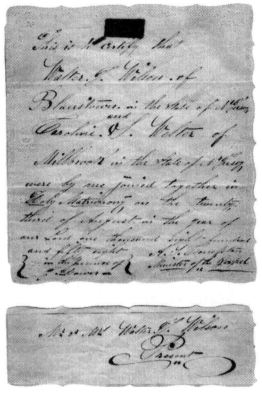

Wedding Certificate of Caroline's 1ˢᵗ marriage

"The name of the Township was Pahaquarry, an Indian name after Chief Paha of the once-famous tribe known as the Delawares." An 1874

Pahaquarry tax survey map shows Conrad Welter owned land in two places, one next to the church/school he founded and the other a little farther out of town.

C. G. Hines followed the Old Mine Road to Pahaquarry. "There are only two villages in the entire township of Pahaquarry, which is nothing but a side hill, anyway, and Millbrook is one of them."

"Here, in 1839, came Coonrad Welter, known to his neighbors as "Coon." His house soon became a home for all the circuit riders and preachers who visited the place, and was known as the "Methodist Tavern." Some of the circuits covered a five hundred mile trail, and the prechers commonly carried a tin horn, with mighty blasts from which they announced their arrival," Hines wrote.

Many of the original roads, such as the Old Mine Road followed Indian trails.

"On Conrad Welter's farm were found many Indian relics, such as spear heads, flints, tomahawks, etc. Along both sides of the Delaware and through Pahaquarry Valley, was at one time the great and famous hunting grounds of the Delaware Indians," family documents say.

"Their hunting grounds seem to have been, as history tells us, from a place now know as Lackawaxen on the Delaware, in Pennsylvania, on the West and in New York and New Jersey on the East."

DELAWARE WATER GAP

"There are historic places near where Conrad Welter lived," ancestors related. "The noted and famous Water Gap on the Delaware, about fourteen miles from his farm and home, also the mountains the Indians called 'Kittatinny' meaning the endless mountain reaching from Maine to Georgia."

"(Conrad's) farm was located on the West and directly at the foot of the Mountains, about one mile from the Delaware River, and about at the head of Pahaquarry Valley, which was very narrow at this place."

"The states of New York, New Jersey and Pennsylvania corner on a rock in midstream of the Delaware river between Milford and Port Jervis. The river approaches the mountains and follows their western side through a succession of mountains, gradually increasing in grandness to the Delaware Water Gap. The country North of the Blue Ridge and above the Gap bore the Indian of Minisink. Here a vast lake probably once extended," ancestors wrote

"To the first settlers these mountains provided a troublesome barrier, and all intercourse southward necessarily passed through the natural gateway of the Gap. In the year 1800, a passable road was made through it by the exertions of the neighbors for their own convenience." documents relate.

SETTLERS' LIFE IN MILLBROOK

The move must have been particularly trying for the pregnant Mary Fulkerson Welter as they bumped over the rough roadways to their new home.

No reference is made to Mary's condition in the family documents, but birth records validate Caroline Welter Wilson Ferrel's birth a few months after the family arrived in Millbrook.

"There was no store or post office, the nearest being a distance of ten miles at a place called Blairstown, named after the great railroad magnate and financier Mr. Blair, who was a warm, personal friend of Mr. Welter, and often helped him financially through his bank at Belvidere," records relate.

"Conrad Welter's four oldest sons, now being young men of good health and strong constitution, entering in with their father as their leader and adviser, with their youthful and manly courage, at once began to fell the forests around them. They soon began to see the fruits of their labors in bountiful harvests," according to his descendants.

"The people of Mill Brook were true pioneer folk, cutting timber and farming the stoney hillsides to earn a meager living," Myra Snook wrote in 1969.

"Tobacco and buckwheat were the main crops raised," Snook wrote, "along with flax and wool. After 1840 broom corn was grown. Flax and wool, usually dyed with Indigo were used for clothing."

"Little money was available," Snooks wrote, "so barter was common." Sometimes it was necessary to trade over the mountain at Flatbrookville. Light farm wagons were used, since heavier conestogas or the cumbersome Jersey wagons couldn't get over the mountain. Travel was mostly by horse or by foot. Because of this, most travel was to the west – Calno and the Delaware River. Rapids in the river made travel hazardous."

Nancy Lynch at grave of Mary Fulkerson

Caroline's mother

An 1860 map of Millbrook shows Coonrad Welter's house between J. Ossenbaugh's and Ben J. Courtright, but the wildlife-laden forests encroached.

"There were animals roaming through the mountain woods that were not pleasant to meet without being armed, such as wolves, bears, panthers, cats and lynx.

"They kept under cover mostly by day but at night they would seek for and carry off small lambs from the farmer's flocks, or visit his chicken house or yard. Another dreaded enemy was rattlesnakes and copperheads, of which there were many," ancestors wrote.

WHAT OUR MILLBROOK ANCESTORS WORE

Our ancestor's only concession to the subject of clothing was a description of shoes. "The hides of his beef cattle and calves, (Conrad) would take to the tannery and... make into such kinds of leather as was required for making boots and shoes for his family."

"(Conrad) would then hire a good, competent shoe maker to come to his house and shoe the entire family for the winter. This would require perhaps from four to six weeks," they wrote.

"Homespun and calico dresses were worn by women and children with matching sunbonnets.

This style was later worn by women of the wagon trains," Snook wrote.

"Men went coatless, hatless and barefooted in summer and wore 'cowhides' on their feet in winter. Usually there was an issue of one new pair of shoes and one new suit per year," Snook wrote.

Although our direct ancestors skipped over the clothing issue, Cummins and Snell wrote at greater length about what people wore, and what they tell us flies in the face of any romanticism we may feel for the old days!

"Style was not in fashion in those days. Women would go on foot for miles dressed in their tidy "homespun" and calico sun-bonnet, and the big girls were not ashamed to dress in the same economical style of their mothers, and, for shoes and stockings, nature furnished them in the summer, while in winter the home-made 'cow-hides' were not a bit too coarse for the genuine young lady of 'ye olden times,'" Snell wrote.

"As for the men, if they went coatless and hatless, with their torn trousers a few inches too short at either end, and their feet as bare as Father Adam's, no exceptions were taken by any one," Snell added.

Cummins wrote that "...everybody went barefoot from April until the snow flew in November. The men often made their feet stand the hard wear better by applying tar to their soles, and then stepping on sand," Snell said.

Deeds -Warren County,N.J.Belvidere

V-50-pp 93-94-95- Dec.24,1859-consideration $1,091.25·-Coonrod
Welter and wife Keziah of Pahaquarry Twp. to Elias L.Garis of Pahaquarry Twp.Land in Pahaquarry Twp. beginning at stone for a
corner in a line of lands of John I.Blair,S & W to stones,then S &
E to stones,S & E to stones a corner to the church lot,then along
said lot,then N & E to the end of the wall of the graveyard,then
along said wall,N & E to a corner of said wall,then S & E to a
large rock at the foot of a steep ledge by a brook,then S & W
to a corner at the north end of a small bridge on the road leading to Millbrook,then S & E to a corner on a bridge on the road
leading over the mountain,then along said road N & E to a corner
at the turn of said road,then N & W to a stake,a corner to James
Ozenbaugh,then N & E to a stone corner to said Ozenbaugh,then N &
W to stones then N & E to stones a corner to said Ozenbaugh in
Abraham Garis line,then N & W to beginning containing 29 & 10/100
acres.

    It being part of the same land which was conveyed to the gran-
tor from Jacob Cummins &wife by deed 4/1/1839-recorded V-18-pp 42
etc.

Recorded 12/31/1859.

Jacob Cummins to Coonrod Welter 4/1/1839

typed copy of deed of land Conrad later sold

back to Jacob Cummins

**"One new suit a year was all that could be
obtained for each person of a family, and this was
all made in the neighborhood," Snell continued.**

"For instance, as late as 1847 Cornelius Carhart would take his wool to a Mr. Ross at Buttzville, who carded it and made it into rolls. It was then spun by Sally Ann Shafer, at the Carhart home, after which it was taken to Effie Axford to be woven into blankets or linsey-woolsey for men's winter trousers, and the finest of it into cloth for the women's dresses, some of which was dyed blue, some left tow color, and some with the warp undyed and the woof dyed blue.

"Or he raised flax and let it lie in the field until rotten, then broke it and hetcheled it. The fine flax was spun by Sally Ann Shafer into sewing thread, and the coarser tow into thread for trousers, the cloth for which was made just wide enough to allow a selvage at the bottom and top of the garment. The linen was dyed with indigo by dipping three times and laying in the sun for a day each time," Snell concluded.

Our Methodist ancestors faced strict clothing regulations to which they also had to adhere or face disciplinary actions.

"Maintaining a dress code further worked to promote Methodist solidarity and communal identity," Wiggers wrote. Ruffles, bows, large hats or bonnets were frowned upon.

"Along with injunctions against swearing, drunkenness, pretentious dress, sexual immorality, and neglecting class meetings, it is worth noting that Methodist preachers were actively interested in promoting such middle class values as cleanliness," Wiggers wrote.

CONRAD WELTER POLITICS AND RELIGION

"Conrad Welter's political views were of the Jacksonian Democracy. He never took any particular or active part in political matters, but was often consulted concerning those who wished to be elected to office and placed in power politically."

Andrew Jackson, who was President from 1828 to 1836, held great appeal for farmers and the middle class of Conrad's time, but was less popular with the establishment.

"After about two years [in Millbrook, Conrad] began to look around him for some means and ways of giving the young members of his family at least a common school education."

"There were no schools, churches or religious meetings of any kind or denomination in this part of the country within ten miles' distance, over the rugged mountains on either side of his humble home," our ancestors wrote.

In his 1882 history of Sussex and Warren County Snell said "No effort previous to 1839 had been made to erect a house of worship in this township, and it was not until Rev. Henry Mains came on this circuit, that the old church and school-house combined was projected."

"Mr. Mains was preceded in 1839 by Rev. Baker, who formed a class at Millbrook, at the house of Coonrad Welter, with Mr. Welter as leader and the members being Mary Welter, Dingman Decker, and wife, and Benjamin Shoemaker and Uriah Hill and wife Sarah Hill," Snell wrote.

Conrad built a chapel with a stone basement, which was occupied for several years as a schoolroom. The upper room also served as a meeting room. It was 'old-fashioned, Methodist plain' our ancestors wrote in the 1900s.

"There were no stained glass windows, no cushioned seats or pews, book-racks or foot-rests, simply plain wooden seats with no back rests; but it was a place where... men and women met to worship God in a true Christian spirit."

"All the materials required to build this chapel was taken from his farm by himself and his helpful sons."

"The first school in this township was in 1840-41. In those years, the Methodists erected a small frame building on the hill near the graveyard at Mill Brook, under which was a basement, built and used for school purpose until 1868," Snell wrote.

"The first teacher in the old basement schoolroom was Edmund L. Gregg," Snell said, and he received about $300 for a nine-month school year. The school was valued at $300 and there were about 45 children.

"When the old church was projected, it became necessary to elect trustees, when Coonrad Welter, Uriah Hill, Dingman Decker and Benjamin Shoemaker were duly elected trustees for the Methodist Society at Mill Brook," Snell wrote.

In the *History of Millbrook,* by Hannah Dickisson Depue, a photo of the church is shown that states proudly that "Millbrook was settled long before other white men pioneered the area."

Any time family reference is made to Conrad Welter, religion is the next word. Family lore claims no one came between Conrad and his God. It's interesting to note that Henricus was born Catholic, and to speculate about what he thought about his son's Methodist campaign.

Religion in general, and Methodism in particular, with its camp meetings during this time, provided a socializing framework in the frontiers, which helped maintain the peace.

"The early Methodist movement had the ability to shape culture and society as well as reflect it, but its influence was not without limitations. Methodism was both driven and constrained primarily by the needs, hopes and fears of ordinary people." Wigger wrote.

Caroline and William Oran Ferrel's wedding certificate

"American Methodism was the largest, most geographically diverse movement of middling and artisan men and women in the early republic," Wigger wrote. The first Methodist church in the area was established in Blairstown in 1838.

"The pioneer preachers in this township, as far as is now known, were Manning Force and George Banghart, who found their way to the seclusion of Pahaquarry in the latter part of the last century or early in that of the present," Snell wrote.

"When Coonrad Welter located in this valley... his home became the preacher's home, and "Coon" Welter's was known as the 'Methodist Tavern,'" Snell said in his 1822 book about Pahaquarry township. Since, according to Wigger, Methodism developed in response to crime, violence and alcohol consumption that tripled today's rate, "Methodist Tavern" is most likely just a slang term in use at the time. Most Methodist meetings at that time were not in churches but were above stores and other establishments, referred to as 'Taverns.'

"The church's Discipline condemned indebtedness, intemperate drinking, swearing, ostentatious dress, gossiping, discord, gluttony, gambling, bribery and taking 'treats' when voting at civil elections..." Wigger wrote.

Coonrad's house "was also one of the preaching-places or 'appointments' on Manning Force and George Banghart's five mile circuit,"

Snell continued. It seems likely that if, in fact, alcohol was served, Coonrad would have lost his exhorter's license.

"The tooting of the itinerant's tin horn" announced his approach to any settlement, and whether the preaching hour was in the afternoon or evening the old 'circuit-rider' was always welcomed by a large gathering of the pioneers for miles around," Wigger wrote.

Methodism, the religion that drove and inspired your ancestors, was first introduced to America when John Wesley visited in 1735 but really began in 1766 with the arrival of Philip Embury from Ireland.

The First General Conference was held in 1792, and the Methodist Protestant Church founded in 1830. The Wesley brand of Methodism was influenced by the Moravian style of evangelism, which they embraced in the United States.

The first Methodist Episcopal church in the area was established in 1838 in Blairstown, New Jersey.

"Conrad Welter was a licensed exhorter and was the leader and father of Methodism in this part of the country," our ancestors wrote.

"(Conrad) was closely associated with Force, then presiding elder for that district who traveled over the rugged mountains for miles on horseback, with saddle bags strapped behind his saddle for weeks at a time when he would make Mr. Welter's house his home, and they would travel for miles around and hold meetings at private houses, and in the groves in warm weather."

Pairing of experienced and inexperienced itinerant preachers was often at the heart of Methodism.

"The development of close personal ties between the preachers formed the foundation of Methodist ministerial training. In many respects the Methodist system was based on the artisan concept of apprenticeship," John Wigger wrote in *Methodism and the Shaping of American Culture,* in 2001.

"Great success attended their works of Christian love and good fellowship. Many were converted to the Christian faith and became good men and women," our ancestors wrote.

"Mr. Welter was a host in prayer and good in exhortation. When he had what he called his good times, he would rise above his calmness, forget his impediments and astonish all that heard him," they said. Unexplained in these documents is what his impediments are. It's one of those unanswerable questions.

Conrad Welter

"At such times there was a sublimity in his language, a force in his manner, and with all an unction attending his discourse overwhelming to the audience."

"An early and thorough education would have made him a mighty man in his day. As it was he used the weapons he had at hand," ancestors said.

Who was it that Conrad spent his life converting and exhorting?

"Methodists drew their converts not only from the unchurched of the western frontiers, but also from the ranks of lapsed New England Congregationalists and nominal southern Episcopalians. Put simply, American Methodism was the largest, most geographically diverse movement of middling and artisan men and women in the early republic," Wiggers wrote.

"There was a pervasive rootlessness to the period (after the Revolutionary War) as many pulled up stakes to move west, or at least psychologically traded traditional concepts of deference for new ideas about democracy and equality," Wiggers wrote

Conrad's family life centered on religion, and his family joined him in prayer every morning before going to work on his farm.

"Before the business of the day was entered upon, he and his family, and all who were within his gates, were called together at the house to join in family worship around the family altar, where he would pour out his heart's thoughts in gratitude to his God for His protecting care and blessings. This was his custom throughout his whole life, ever believing and acknowledging the hand of his God in all things," ancestors wrote.

Evidently, our early-1900s ancestors were as impressed by morning family prayers as we are today. But for the Methodists of the time this was not optional. Daily prayer was one of the disciplines of the early Methodist church, which began to lose its clarity in the late 1800s.

Such daily involvement of religion in family life at the time was extended to the children.

"The Church and Sunday Schools at this time were several, within a short distance of each other. The young people and many of the older people would take active part in these religious exercises," our ancestors wrote of the continuing importance of religion in the Welter lives.

"These different schools often met together and received good religious instructions from the older of those that were considered competent to give such instruction."

"As a rule, the people were religiously inclined. The young people seemed to be drawn to these meetings, not out of idle curiosity but to receive good instructions religiously," our ancestors concluded.

ESTABLISHING A MAIL ROUTE AND STAGE COACH

In addition to contributing to the growth of religion and education in Millbrook, "Conrad Welter was the first one who proposed a mail route from Columbia on the Jersey shore of the Delaware to Flatbrookville, through Pahaquarry Valley.

"He and a few others of his neighbors" petitioned Washington, D.C. and the route was granted to Millbrook and about 30 other villages in the area in about 1851. "There were several small post offices along this mail route. The distance to be carried was about fifteen miles, ending in Flatbrookville, and the mail was delivered by carrier once a week."

"The mail carrier very often had to be postmaster as well for often, when he would arrive at the office with the mail pouch (there never was but one pouch) the Postmaster was away, perhaps out in the fields on his farm attending to his crops, and to save time, the carrier would unlock the pouch, sort the mail and go to the next office where he would have to do the same trick over," writers relate.

"The compensation for carrying the mail was small. The carrier would very often have a passenger to take on the way who he charged a small fee, which usually went for a good dinner at a place called Columbia Station."

"A few years later," our ancestors wrote, "a mail and stage route was established between Newton and Flatbrookville. Newton, at that time, was the terminal of the New York and Midland Railroad. Jesse T. Welter was the owner of this stage route and carried the mails for several years through Millbrook," our ancestors wrote.

From a diagram Myra Snooks drew, in the 1880s the little village of Mill Brook was a bustling town that boasted a hotel; a weaver, Mrs. Kimble; next to a blacksmith, Isaac Kimble; Atwood Garris, a shoemaker; and a grist mill.

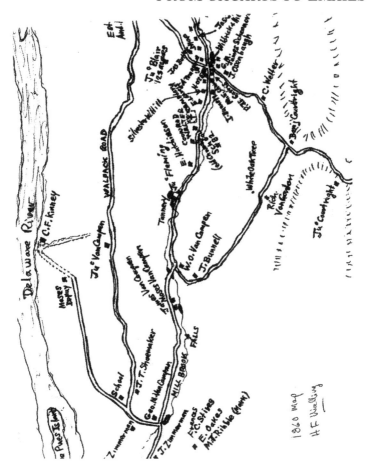

1860 Map of Millbrook Village

MILLBROOK FARM LIFE

The first five or six years Conrad devoted to clearing the land while raising enough grains and stock for his needs. After that, he became a very successful farmer and his farm life duties are detailed in the documents.

"As he gradually cleared his land, he became more independent, for the land was of a very rich soil, and it produced fine crops of grain and hay."

"His livestock increased also, so that by the year 1849 he had a fine stock of cattle, horses, sheep and hogs, so that he became quite independent, so far as being self-supporting."

"It was necessary for him to cut quite a large amount of grass for hay, for his stock was increasing yearly. This was also done by hand with stick and scythe. After being dried in the field, it was raked up in winrows and hauled to the barns or place of stacking."

"He would then take his flock of sheep to the creek and place them in a corral which he built in a circle with one side opening into the creek, and about the first of May he would take them one by one into the water and thoroughly wash their fleeces of wool on their backs.

"They were then turned out into a clean meadow pasture until they were thoroughly dry, and then they were sheared by hand.

"The wool was either sent to the factory or made into rolls for spinning into yarn for woolen stockings for the family. The carding and spinning was done by the women folks. A spinning wheel was a necessity in every household."

"His flax crop was gathered with great care. Very often the younger members of his family would pull up the entire crop, bind it into small bundles and shock it. When good and thoroughly dried, the seed would be threshed out by hand, the straw laid out on the ground to rot the stock, then it would be taken up and put through a hand brake so that the stock would loosen from the fiber.

"It was then hetcheled over an iron-tooth homemade contrivance for the purpose. It was then sent to the factory and made into linen cloth for the use of the family in the summer months.

Sugar was also home-grown. "From his sugar maple trees on his farm, he would gather sap in the spring of the year by tapping the trees. He then boiled the sap down into good maple syrup, enough for his own use, then would boil considerable more down to a very good, dry brown sugar.

Nine years after the Welters moved to Millbrook, Mary Fulkerson died from complications from the birth to her last son, Henry, leaving Caroline, the only girl, in charge of her siblings.

"Mary Fulkerson Welter was a true Christian mother, devoted to her husband and family, and with her Christian example sought to teach her family the true principles of Christian living, and when lying on her last bed of sickness (she) called her children one by one to her bedside and exhorted them to give their hearts to God, and to follow the example set before them by a Christian father and mother whose aim had been to live a simple Christian life, and to show before the world true Christian love and good fellowship."

Millbrook village sign

MILLBROOK SOCIAL LIFE

"After about ten years, this little valley was well filled with settlers. Farm joined farm that was well tilled, and they were all quite prosperous, happy and contented," Conrad's descendants wrote.

"Everyone seemed willing and anxious to serve his neighbor in any way possible, and they seemed to be content and happy as one family," ancestors wrote.

"Being entirely away from any places of amusements, they would visit each other in the winter months and have their afternoon teas, especially the heads of the families,"

"Great quantities of nuts grew throughout this valley, such as walnuts, white hickory nuts and chestnuts, which were gathered by the younger members of the families until there was a large store laid up for winter use.

"Very often each member of the family had their own private stock of nuts laid up the purpose of treating their young friends in the long winter evenings."

"There were a goodly number of young people in the valley, ranging in age from fourteen to twenty. They would have their home parties and all were invited.

"There were no musicals or theatre parties for them to attend. These were unknown to them, so that they had to amuse themselves as best they could," ancestors related.

"There were no cliques. No one thought himself or herself better than his neighbor, but they would come together as one family at some invited house of their neighbors, would spend the evening socially on these occasions, the nuts and

81

cider would be handed around freely, they would have their simple and harmless plays, and before the hour of midnight they would bid their hostess good night and return to their homes smiling and happy.

"It must be remembered that, on these pleasant occasions, the young gentleman would see his best girl home from the party, which made it very agreeable and pleasant for both," ancestors coyly wrote.

"There were also horseback parties on a pleasant Sunday afternoon for a ten- or fifteen-mile ride. There were some expert lady riders. Some place would be announced as their starting point, and from thence they would couple off for a nice gallop to some particular place of interest," they said.

"Many of the social events of the 1800s centered around a necessary phase of life," Snook concurred. "The ordinary chore was made into an event in which friends and neighbors entered. These usually gave way to dancing to the tune of a violin or to games, in most of which were kissing."

"The community was dependent in its amusements, as in everything else, entirely on itself," Cummins wrote in stressing the utilitarian aspects of Warren County social life.

"It lost no opportunity, therefore, to gain entertainment from the commonest affairs of life, so that every gathering, for any purpose, was distinctly a social event," Cummins said.

"One of these was a quilting party, at which the ladies worked all day quilting one of those matchless creations containing thousands of pieces, while the men appeared in time for supper, which was followed by a social evening," Cummins wrote.

"A 'Stone Frolic' gathered all the men of the neighborhood to picking the loosed stones from a new ground while the ladies were preparing a feast for them at the house. A 'Raising,' socially, was about the same thing, but the work consisted in raising the frame of a new building. Husking bees, plowing frolics and the like were usually to aid some neighbor, who, owing to sickness, was behind with his work.

"Apple cuts" were a form of useful diversion at which apples were peeled, cored and quartered in preparation for drying on scaffolds erected for that purpose.

"After eleven o'clock the apple paring gave way to games such as 'Steal the partners,' 'Candid,' and 'Top,' in most of which kissing entered somewhere, or to dancing to the music of a violin which was the common musical instrument before 1850," Cummins concluded.

The farmers often made "husking bees, as they were called, after the corn was cut and stood in shock. At the proper time he would invite his

Nancy Ott Lynch

neighbors, old and young, on some bright moonlit night to come to his husking bee," our ancestors wrote.

"On these occasions, the neighbors would all turn out of a good time, and would husk out perhaps his entire crop. After a couple of hours husking, they would return to the house and partake of the good things provided by the ladies.

"The older ones would then retire and leave the field clear for the youngsters who would have a good time for an hour, perhaps, or sometimes longer," ancestors wrote.

According to Myra Snooks, whoever found "a red ear got a kiss."

Photos of restored Millbrook Village

COONRAD SELLS HIS LAND

Maps indicate that Coonrad deeded some of his land to the Church and to his son Jacob, then Coonrad and his second wife Kaziah sold some remaining land, almost 30 acres, to Elias L. Garis of Pahaquarry on December 24, 1859, for $1,091.25.

In a registered deed the land was said to begin "at stones for a corner in a line of lands of John I. Blair, S and W to stones, then S and E to stones at corner to the church lot, then along said lot, then N&E to the end of the wall of the graveyard, then along said wall, N&E to a corner of said wall, then S&E to a large rock at the foot of a steep ledge by a brook, then S&W to a corner at the north end of a small bridge on the road leading to Millbrook, then S&E to a corner on a bridge on the road leading over the mountain, then along said road N&E to a corner at the turn of said road, then N&W to a stake, a corner to James Ozenbaugh, then N&E to stones a corner to said Ozenbaugh in Abraham Garis line, then N&W to beginning containing 29&10/100 acres, "it being part of the same land which was conveyed to the grantor from Jacob Cummins and wife by deed 4/1/1839.

The graveyard, brook and road over the mountain were the only points easily found in a visit to the restored Millbrook village in 2003. However, four shade saplings planted around the perimeter of where Conrad's house had stood are just gaining venerability.

CAROLINE'S STORY

In 1848, when she was nine years old, Caroline took charge of her siblings – seven-year-old Benjamin, four-year-old Rebecca, and infant Henry, whose birth led to his mother's death.

Caroline's older sister Margaret died in infancy, but at the time of her mother's death the rest of her family included older brothers Elijah, Jesse, Joseph, Jacob, Charles, Asa, and Isaiah.

The following year Conrad wed a local widow, Kaziah Rifenberry, and John was born in July 1849, Abraham in January 1852, Theodore in 1855, and Mary in 1878, further crowding the tiny home.

Henry only lived four years after his mother's death, dying July 1852 of unknown causes. Caroline's oldest brother Elijah died in a train crash in August of that same year.

Three years before the start of the Civil War, and ten years after her mother's death, Caroline wed Walter J. Wilson of Blairstown, New Jersey.

"Mr. Wilson was a successful farmer near Dallas, Pennsylvania, where he moved soon after their marriage," and "he soon became well known through that part of Luzerne County for his uprightness and honesty. His political opinions were Democratic. He was nominated and elected to the State Senate from his Congressional District."

Tragically, on November 1, 1876, "He was taken down at the beginning of his political campaign with typhoid fever and died on the day of his election. Thus ended the career of one who had been a good husband and kind father," family documents relate.

"Conrad retired from his farm life and went to Wyoming Valley, Pennsylvania to spend the remaining days with his sons and daughters. He lived to the age of 88 when he died in the full triumph of his Christian faith, assuring his many friends that all would be well with him in the hereafter," his ancestors wrote. Hopefully his support was helpful to the widowed Caroline.

"Thus the lamp of life went out for one who had been a kind father and true Christian. His remains were laid to rest in the cemetery at Dallas, Pennsylvania," the manuscript records.

Five years after Caroline's first husband died, she married William Oran Ferrel, and their son Ralph Winfield Ferrel was born May 18, 1882, when Caroline was 43. William was in his fifties when his last son was born.

1st page of William Oran Ferrel's handwritten narrative

THE FERREL FAMILY'S BEGINNINGS
IN THE UNITED STATES

"I cannot go back with my ancestry (on) my Father's side (any further) than to the settlement of Ireland by three Sons of King of Spain. He fitted them out with three ships. The first one that landed in Ireland was to (be) head of affairs, but when they got ready (to) sail they got aboard 1 ship so that neither 1 should have the advantage. That is the reason they stick together," William O. Ferrel wrote in the family Bible.

The seventh of twelve children, Billy O. "was born (in) Cornwall Township, Orange County, New York, April 18, 1827 in a log house." Billy brags that all 12 children grew into adulthood, something truly unusual at the time.

"Whether my father was emigrated from Ireland or Spain, history is silent, or at what date, but they settled in N.J." Billy O. continued.

How William didn't know whether his father was from Ireland or Spain, especially since it's clear from his narrative that he had heard his father tell stories, is just another unanswerable historical question.

William O. recorded his Ferrel family history on March 2, 1911, with an elegant hand. William was known as "Billy O." While some descendants believed that the "O" stood for O'Ferrel, in fact, Billy's middle name was Oran. Where the name Oran came from is another mystery. Maybe it derived from Orange County where they settled, or a misspelling of the more common name Orin?

"My father David C. and one brother, William, settled in Orange County, New York." Billy O. tells us.

"In early life my father used to trap and hunt on the head waters of the Hudson. In the winter when Indians were plenty I have heard him tell of some escapes. In summer he worked on board of sailboats. Was soldier in the war of 1812 on the Canada line," Billy O. said.

Not much was written in the family documents about Billy's mother, Rachel Roberts, other than she was buried in South Eaton, Pennsylvania.

Billy's grandfather, Rachel's father, fled the 'Wyoming Massicree' "taking with him such of his belongings as he could pack on horse with his wife and a pack on back and driving a cow on foot through Cobs Gap to the Delaware River near Carpenters Point." They survived on milk and grain for six weeks.

More than 3,000 residents fled the area as a result of the July 3, 1778, Wyoming Valley event, a Revolutionary War battle that ended when the British regulars, Tories and Indians overwhelmed American forces. Invaders killed many farmers and houses, crops and cattle were destroyed.

Both the Welter and Ferrel families were involved in this incident. The Ferrel settlers were fleeing the battle and drummer boy Henry Welter was with General Sullivan's forces responding to the 'massacre' by razing Iroquois villages, orchards and crops. Much of the homeland of the Six Nations was destroyed in this retaliatory campaign.

BILLY O'S LIFE

Billy, was born during John Quincy Adams's last year as President, and his earliest memories began during Andrew Jackson's Presidency.

Billy recalls "when we moved to a tenant house on John Miller's farm." Two roads led to the farm and he remembered "the wagon containing most of the furniture going around the hill whilst Mother drove the oxen to a sled up over the hill on a shorter rout. I can remember distinctly of riding on the sled and holding fast to stakes stuck in a hole board in a bench of the sled, although I was but three years old."

When Billy was about five he was sent to board for two years with Mr. Miller. "They were Methodist, but Mr. Miller got to drinking. Mrs. Miller was afraid that he might do me harm so she sent me home," Billy wrote.

After a month at home Billy was sent to live for several months with an old Revolutionary soldier, Michael Smith, who lived four miles away in Newberg, the principal city in Orange County at the time.

Michael Smith's family "had friends living in N.Y.," Billy wrote, "They rigged me up in a new suit of clothes, boots and a high silk hat and sent me home. Wasn't I something?" Billy reminisced.

When Billy was five, he "moved to Warwick Township, a residential area. I was there a few weeks, then I went to live with Mr. James Gray where I (spent) the happiest years of my boyhood. They were Presbyterians. I worked for my board and clothes and three months' schooling each year. I had learned (to) read and was a bookworm," Billy said.

The Gray family "kept the Township Library. I (had) access to all the books I wanted, comprising almost ancient history together with the lives (of) Mohamed, Hannibal, Napoleon, Washington and hosts of other prominent men. Here I graduated (from Apprenticeship) at thirteen. What little (education) I have came by practice," He added.

Ralph Winfield Ferrel - Caroline's last son - my grandfather

In addition to the classics Billy would have found politics interesting reading, with the presidency changing hands often during his youth. In 1836 Martin Van Buren began his one term as president, and then in 1840 William Henry Harrison was elected and served one year. John Tyler was elected in 1841 and served until 1844.

"In the fall of 1840 when I was 13 [we came] from Warwick Orange Co. to Thurston Holow, Pa, Arriving there quite stiff from my long walk [about 88 miles]. We had no public schools at that (time) and was too poor to pay tuition." That year Billy O worked on a farm, and in the winter he and his mother worked at weaving "as much as five yards per day" of cloth. At night he read by the light of pine nuts.

Illumination was a challenge in those days, according to George Wyckoff Cummins in 1911. One early form of lighting was the tallow dip.

A tallow dip candle was "made by dipping a cotton wick a number of times into melted tallow until it was large enough to suit one's fancy. They usually measured about eight inches long by three quarters of an inch in a diameter. Sometimes if candles were not forthcoming, the most primitive lamp was used…"

"It consisted of a flat earthen dish containing lard, and reaching from this to the edge of the dish was a bit of twisted cotton cloth for a wick.

This was lighted, and gave about as much light as a tallow dip." Early historian Cummins wrote.

Of course, lighting these devices depended on embers which were kept live in the fireplace, and Cummins remembered the repercussions if the fireplace went cold.

"If that fire went out, my mother, for instance, had to go to the nearest neighbors... a quarter mile away, to get a red-hot piece of charcoal, which she brought back, covered with ashes, to start the fire again," Cummins said.

In 1840 Billy O. "worked for William Conklin about 3 miles from Goshen [the geographical center of Orange County and about ten miles from Warwick] in sight of the line of the Erie RR then in construction." The track was finished that fall as far as Goshen.

"Goshen, 'the promised land' was first known by the name Goshen in 1714, but had its boundaries established in 1788... it was incorporated in 1809,"Hope Farm Press wrote. "It is the principal shipping point for milk from the large and fertile surrounding dairy section..."

Billy wrote, "I was at Goshen the day the first passenger train came up from Piermont with 500 passengers from N.Y. to a free dinner. The train was expected at 11 o'clock but (did) not arrive until about 4 on account of a short curve some 6 miles below. They (did) not understand that the out track had to (be) raised. This was (a) red-letter day but some got hungry. The hotels made preparations for passengers. Sightseers could get nothing to eat. Some came from fifty miles."

The establishment of a railroad from New York to Goshen paved the way for new commerce. The first milk shipped into New York City came from Goshen, and Goshen butter became famous.

Railroad construction had an enormous impact on your immediate ancestors. Conrad Welter was friendly with John I. Blair, who Welter descendants claimed "was successful in buying the right-of-way through New Jersey and Pennsylvania to Scranton for the DL&W RR. This was the first 'road' from New York to Scranton, a distance of about 168 miles. The first trains were run about the year 1855," they wrote.

Billy O. wrote that "in the spring of 1844, I and my brother David took a small drove of cattle from Thurston Holow to Orange Co., consign to friends there. They paying our expenses. I got a position with a farmer at $4.50 per month which I thought fair wages as some men got no more. That was the fall of the Polk election," Billy O. related.

"That fall I came home and hired with my brother Nathaniel to work at Mason work for 3 years, 1 year at $25 dollars, 2 years at $35 and 3 at $50. In the spring of 1845 I took another small drove to Orange Co., then moved there during his apprenticeship."

"Then I worked in N.J. one summer, coming home in the fall of 1848 just before my father's death. Made my home with my mother working at my trade in summer, threshing grain in winter. While in Orange Co., winters I cut cord wood."

Some other memorable natural events in Billy's life included when, in the fall of 1834, he "saw the stars fall." "We staid up quite late to see them, but the greatest display was about 3 o'clock in the morning."

"In 1835 and 1836 was what was called as the hard winter. Snow was full four foot deep in fields. After it settled by rain it had a crust so that they teamed on it over fences," Billy wrote.

"In 1837 I was in a field one afternoon when it began to grow dark. It grew so that it looked like night. I did (not) know what to think of it. People said that hens went to roost, though it was not more than 2 or 3 o'clock. Caused by total eclipse of the sun."

"The winter following there was such a display of northern lights on a bright moonlight night that the snow looked like blood," Billy remembered.

From the time he was 14 religion factored heavily in Bill O's life. Word of Methodist conferences was spread by horseback and "meetings," which were a primary source of entertainment and civilizing influence in the early to mid 1800s.

"In (the) winter of forty-one and two Elisha and Daniel Harris and Henry Face came to Thurston Holow and held a series of meetings. At these meetings scores were converted, of whom (I) am the only one left. The rest have gone to their rewards," Billy wrote.

Caroline and William Oran Ferrel's wedding certificate

On the Fourth of July, 1850, Billy O. married Malviney Ide. The couple bore six children.

In 1878 Malviney died, and on January 13, 1881 Billy O. married a widow, Mrs. C. S. Welter Wilson. The couple bore one son, Ralph Winfield, who was your Nana Ott's father. Ralph Winfield Ferrel was my "grandpa."

"I am still striving to serve the Lord in my weakeness. I have ben class leader, steward or trustee and treasurer for the last 30 years," Billy O. concluded in his memoirs.

Class leaders were not self-appointed. "Class leaders were usually lay men and women chosen or approved by the itinerant preacher in charge of the circuit of city station," Wiggers wrote. "class leaders tended to be the more successful and respected members of their neighborhoods and villages."

"In New York City, the majority of class leaders in 1812 were small masters, journeymen, master craftsmen and shopkeepers," Wiggers wrote.

Methodist disciplines encouraged hard work, according to Wiggers.

"Methodists thoroughly embraced and helped to create this new (work) ethic. 'Be diligent. Never be unemployed. Never be triflingly employed,' urged the church's book of Discipline. 'No idleness is consistent with a growth in grace,'"

Wiggers wrote.

FERREL WELTER FAMILY

September 7, 1904, Caroline's son, Ralph Winfield Ferrel, a church organist and writer for *Luzerne Record* newspaper, married Elizabeth Gertrude Jones, a graduate of the Wyoming Seminary class of 1901.

Elizabeth's brother French Jones and Howard Frantz, a nephew of the groom, were attendants at the ceremony, which, oddly enough, given the family's religious backgrounds, was in a private house.

Newspaper clippings describing the event were pasted in a Bible Elizabeth's mother gave her Christmas 1904.

"One of the prettiest weddings of the west side took place last evening when Miss Elizabeth Jones and Ralph W. Ferrel of the *Record* staff, were united in marriage by Rev. Clinton B. Henry, pastor of the Luzerne borough Methodist Church at the home of Mrs. David Prutzman of 418 Charles Street, Luzerne Borough," news clippings report.

"The bride made a charming appearance in a gown of white chiffon trimmed with a valenciennes lace, while in her hair were several large bride roses.

"As the bride and groom came down the stairs Professor David Davies of Dorranceton played the "Lohengrin Wedding March" and during the ceremony "Hearts and Flowers."

"A wedding supper followed, after which the happy couple took a train for Buffalo from which place they will go to St. Louis. They will return in two weeks and will reside at the home of the groom's parents in Luzerne Borough.

"The groom is one of the popular young men of the West Side and was organist at the Luzerne M.E. Church

Another paper wrote about one of the first September weddings on the West Side:

"The nuptial knot was tied amid a charming environment. The home was decorated with autumn leaves and plants, as well as an abundance of cut flowers, and the ceremony which was witnessed by about one hundred relatives and friends was performed in a rear parlor before a large bay window which was decorated with autumn leaves, hydrangeas, potted plants and spruce while overhead hung a large bell."

Ralph and Elizabeth had three girls, Lucille, who married Clark Brown and had one son Russell; Dorothy Elizabeth who married Harry Kenyon and had no children; and Bettina Rose who married Gilbert Russell Ott and had two children, Gilbert Russell Ott, Jr., and Nancy Gail Ott.

FERREL/WELTER BOOK SOURCES

1- Original Ferrel and Welter documentation copyrighted by Nancy Ott Lynch 1997.

2- HistoryCentral.com

3- Worcester Polytechnic Institute Website

4- Columbia County Historical and Genealogical Society, Bloomsberg, Pa.

5- Millbrook Historical Society

6- Diary of a Pahaquarry Farmer, 1861, United States Department of the Interior. Ribble family

7- *Don't Know Much About History*, Kenneth C. Davis

8- Yahoo Reference Columbia Encyclopedia

9- *The German American*, Richard O'Conner

10- Fager's Orange County

11- Church of Latter Day Saints

12- National Park Service - Delaware Water Gap

13- Millbrook Historical Society

14- Wyoming Historical and Geological Society

15- *Sussex andWarren History,* James P. Snell, 1882

16- *History of Warren County, N.J.,* George Wyckoff Cummins

17- *FW Beers and Company County Atlas,* Warren, N.J., 1874

18- Webster's 1828 Dictionary, Electronic Version by Christian Technologies.

19- The Welters Website

20- Statehousegirls.net, New Jersey History

21- *Orange County Cities and Towns,* Hope Farm Press, Saugerties, N.Y.

22- Warren County Regional Chamber of Commerce, "New Jersey's Great Northwest Skylands"

23- *Taking Heaven by Storm,* John H. Wigger

24- *Methodism and the Shaping of American Culture,* John H. Wigger

25- *The Old Mine Road,* C. Gilbert Hine, 1859

26- *History of Mill Brook,* Myra Snook, 1969

27- *Philip Garis Day Book,* Millbrook, N.J., 1874-1876

ABOUT THE AUTHOR

A journalism major and graduate of Southern Methodist University, in Dallas, Texas, Nancy began her writing career at the Associated Press in Miami, Florida.

Her first book is a gift of history for her family.

Lightning Source UK Ltd.
Milton Keynes UK
UKHW010619270123
416054UK00002B/476